Imagine! Oxford Read and Imagine
Beginner

A Nice Book

By Paul Shipton
Illustrated by Steve Cox
Activities by Hannah Fish

Contents

Hello!
My name is Rosie.
Hello!
My name is Ben.

This is Grandpa.
Hello!
Now let's read this story, A Nice Book.

Rosie and Ben are at the library with Grandpa.

They are looking at the books.

'I want a book, please,' says Clunk.

'What books do you like?' says Grandpa.

'I don't know,' says Clunk.

Go to page 15 for activities.

Rosie sits down with a book.

'What are you reading, Rosie?' says Clunk.

'It's a nice book with a horse in it,' says Rosie.

'I don't like books with animals,' says Clunk.

Go to page 16 for activities.

Ben sits down with a book.

'What are you reading, Ben?' says Clunk.

'It's a nice book with a big ship in it,' says Ben.

'I like ships,' says Clunk.

Go to page 17 for activities.

‘And there are pirates in my book,’ says Ben.

‘PIRATES!’ says Clunk. ‘I don’t like pirates!’

Clunk is scared.
He jumps up and
hits Grandpa.

Go to page 18 for activities.

There are books on the floor.

'Sorry, Grandpa,' says Clunk.
'I can pick up your books!'

Then ...

'I like this book!' says Clunk. 'It has a robot in it!'

Go to page 19 for activities.

Activities before you read

Talk **Look at the front cover of this book. Answer the questions and talk to a friend.**

1 What can you see?

2 How many books does Grandpa have?

3 Do you like books?

1 Trace the words. Then match.

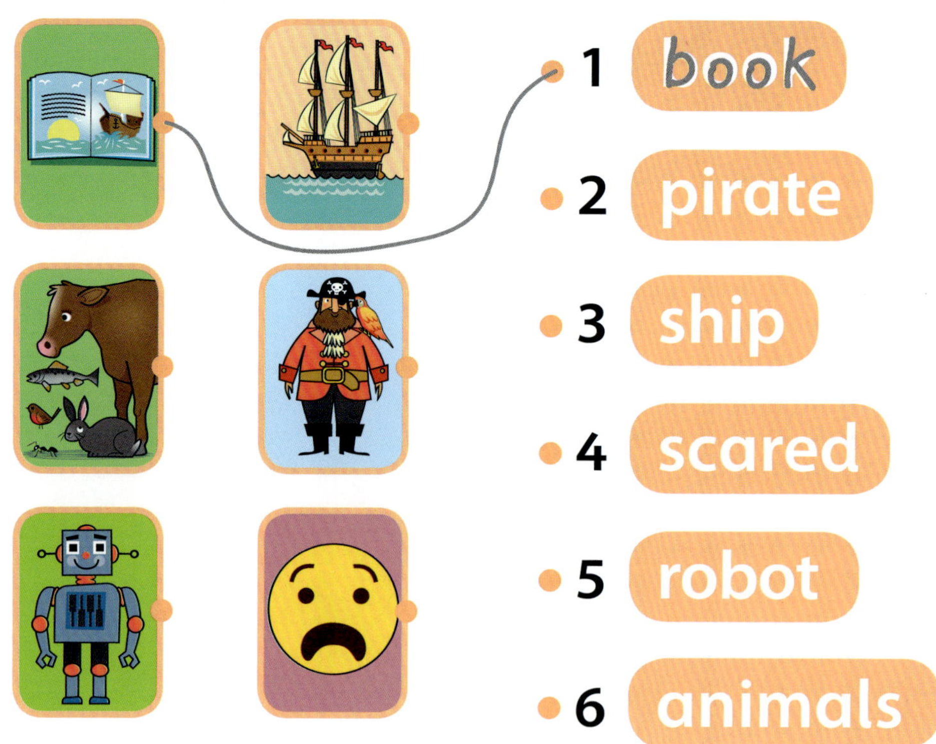

Activities for pages 4–5

1 Choose and write the correct words.

[1] Grandpa, Ben, and Rosie are at the [2] ____________. They are looking at the [3] ____________. [4] ____________ wants a book, too.

Rosie library Clunk books ~~Grandpa~~

2 Circle the correct words.

1 Ben and Rosie are **for** / **at** the library.

2 They are **look** / **looking** at the books.

3 Clunk says, 'I want **book** / **a book**, please.'

4 Grandpa says, 'What books **you** / **do you** like?'

Talk **Do you go to the library? Talk to a friend.**

Activities for pages 6–7

1 Write the words.

1 sit down

tsi wnod

2 ________

roshe

3 ________

linamsa

4 ________

gedanir

2 Trace the words. Then complete the sentences.

book animals ~~sits down~~

1 Rosie sits down with a book.

2 It is a ________ with a horse in it.

3 Clunk doesn't like books with ________.

Talk **Do you like books with animals? Talk to a friend.**

Activities for pages 8–9

1 **Look at the picture on page 8. Write *yes* or *no*.**

1 Ben has a book. yes
2 Clunk is talking to Ben. ______
3 Clunk has a blue bag. ______
4 Grandpa has two books. ______
5 Grandpa has red shoes. ______

2 **Match.**

1 Ben sits down	reading, Ben?'
2 'What are you	ships.
3 Ben's book has	with a book.
4 Clunk likes	a ship in it.

Talk **Do you like books with ships? Talk to a friend.**

Activities for pages 10–11

1 **Put a tick (✓) or a cross (X) in the box.**

1  This is a pirate.  ✓

2  This is scared. 

3  This is hit. 

4  This is Clunk. 

5  This is Ben. 

6  This is jump up. 

Talk **Do you like books with pirates? Talk to a friend.**

Activities for pages 12–13

1 Look at the picture on page 12. Answer the questions.

1 Where are they? in the library

2 How many books are on the floor? ____________

3 What color are Ben's shoes? ____________

4 Is Clunk happy? ____________

2 Trace the words. Then match.

1 floor

2 book

3 pick up

4 robot

Talk Do you like this story? Talk to a friend.

Project Favorite Books

1 Look at the picture and think about the story. Complete the sentences.

1 Grandpa and the children are ____________________.

2 Rosie likes books with ____________________.

3 Ben likes books with ____________________.

4 Clunk likes books with ____________________.

Talk **What books do you like? Talk to a friend.**

2 **What is your favorite book? Draw a picture of the book.**

3 **Now answer the questions about your favorite book.**

1 What is the name of the book? ______________

2 Who writes the book? ______________

3 What is the book about? ______________

____

____

Talk **Show your picture to your friend. Now tell them about your favorite book.**

Picture Dictionary

 animals	 book	 floor	 hit
 horse	 jump up	 library	 look
 pick up	 pirate	 reading	 robot

scared ship sit down

Draw and write your favorite word.

Oxford Read and Imagine

Oxford Read and Imagine graded readers are at nine levels (Early Starter, Starter, Beginner, and Levels 1 to 6) for students from age 3 or 4 and older. They offer great stories to read and enjoy.

Activities provide Cambridge Young Learners Exams preparation. See Key below.

At Levels 1 to 6, every storybook reader links to an **Oxford Read and Discover** non-fiction reader, giving students a chance to find out more about the world around them, and an opportunity for Content and Language Integrated Learning (CLIL).

For more information about **Read and Imagine**, and for Teacher's Notes, go to www.oup.com/elt/teacher/readandimagine

For a free Audio download of the story in a choice of American and British English, go to www.oup.com/elt/readandimagine

  Activity supports Cambridge Young Learners Starters Exam preparation

OXFORD
UNIVERSITY PRESS

Great Clarendon Street, Oxford, OX2 6DP, United Kingdom

Oxford University Press is a department of the University of Oxford. It furthers the University's objective of excellence in research, scholarship, and education by publishing worldwide. Oxford is a registered trade mark of Oxford University Press in the UK and in certain other countries

First published in 2017
2025
12

ISBN: 978 0 19 470909 5

Printed in China

This book is printed on paper from certified and well-managed sources.

ACKNOWLEDGEMENTS

Main illustrations by: Steve Cox.

Additional illustrations by: Dusan Pavlic/Beehive Illustration, Alan Rowe, Mark Ruffle.